Contents

2	Introduction
4	History
14	The Castle Interior
28	Introduction to Glenveagh Castle Gardens
31	Development of the Garderns
40	The Garden Trail

Site Map - Inside Back Cover

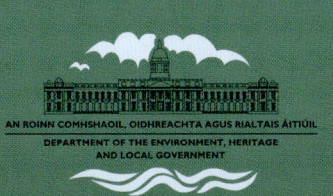

Introduction

Glenveagh Castle is a 19th century castellated mansion, built between 1867 and 1873 in the 'Scottish Baronial' style made famous by Queen Victoria's Scottish retreat at Balmoral. Its construction in a remote mountain setting was inspired by the Victorian idyll of a romantic highland retreat. Similar castellated mansions were constructed in remote scenic areas in the west of Ireland in the 19th century. Most notable of these are Kylemore Castle (now Kylemore Abbey), built by the Manchester financier Mitchell Henry, and Ashford Castle, completed for Sir Arthur Guinness in 1870.

Prior to 1800, the Glenveagh Valley was a wild and uninhabited part of Donegal. The name Glenveagh comes from the Irish, Gleann Bheatha, the Glen of the Birch, an illusion to the predominance of the native tree, Downy Birch, (*Betula pubescens*), which thrives in the acid peaty soil of the area.

History

The early 19th century was a tragic time for the majority of Irish people who lived in appalling conditions of poverty. The peasantry lived in overcrowded conditions, was half-starved and often oppressed by landlords or their agents. The blackest depths of misery were reached following 1845 when the potato crop failed in successive years and the Great Famine ensued. More than a million people in Ireland starved to death or died of disease and a million more emigrated.

Following the Famine, the tenant farmers remained at the mercy of their landlords and could be evicted at will. Their troubles were compounded by the introduction of black-faced mountain sheep from Scotland in the 1850's. A number of Donegal landlords annexed upland areas, which had formerly been commonage and stocked them with sheep. Tenant farmers suddenly found that they were being denied the right to take their livestock to the hills for the summer months, as they had been doing for generations. In Glenveagh, the tenants fell foul of John George Adair.

John George Adair, of a minor landed family, was born in 1823 and inherited his family holdings, the Bellegrove Estate near Ballybrittas, County Laois, (then known as the Queen's County). He transformed his fortune during a career of adventurous land speculation and mortgaging and also bought land in the Encumbered Estates Court, which was established after the Famine to recover debts from bankrupt landlords.

History

Adair first saw Glenveagh in 1857 while on a tour of the area and, in his own words, he was *'enchanted by the surpassing beauty of the scenery'*. After his visit, he immediately began purchasing tracts of land to make a single parcel of some 30,000 acres (11,300 hectares), with the intention of turning it into a hunting estate. A conflict of interest arose between Adair's plans and the needs of the subsidence farming families within the estate. The culmination of this conflict occurred in 1861 when 46 families involving 244 people were evicted from the estate.

Initially, Adair used a small hunting lodge, known as Glenveagh Cottage, located in the upper part of the glen opposite Astellan waterfall. Only the foundation stones of this building can be seen today. In the middle of the 1860's, with plans in train to build a castle at Glenveagh, Adair looked to new business opportunities in America, and increased his fortune still further there through brokerage and ranching. While in the United States, he met a wealthy young widow, Cornelia Ritchie (née Wadsworth, from Geneseo, New York) whose husband had died during the American Civil War.

Cornelia Adair

Sketch of Glenveagh Castle by Townsend Trench

John George Adair

They married in Paris in 1867 and returned to Bellegrove, where Adair remodelled the house for his wife. In 1868-69, he started on the construction of Glenveagh Castle, which was designed by John Townsend Trench, a cousin of Adair's. The Castle was sited on a small promontory jutting into Lough Veagh, with fine views along the glen. It was designed to resemble Balmoral on a reduced scale, and duly included a four-storey rectangular keep with turrets. The designer also appears to have imitated the style of earlier Irish towerhouses, which over the years had acquired lower, less defensive and more modern extensions as can be seen at Donegal Castle in the south of the county.

Glenveagh Castle under construction c.1871

The building stone chosen was granite, plentiful in Donegal but difficult to work and allowing for little detail. The final effect depended largely on the bold keep tower with its distinctively stepped battlements, a feature discovered by antiquarians of the period to be peculiar to Ireland. A few roughly medieval details, including corner turrets or bartizans with decorative arrow-loops and a crowning mock watchtower enliven the silhouette of the keep. However, the castle's greatest distinction remains its setting.

In the 1870's, the Adairs began to spend increasing amounts of time in America, where they developed new business interests and travelled extensively. In 1875, Adair moved his brokerage to Denver, Colorado, and the following year founded his most successful business, the J.A. Ranch, in the Palo Duro Canyon, Texas. On his way home from a third visit to the ranch in 1885, Adair died suddenly in St. Louis, Missouri. His wife thereafter paid an annual autumn visit to the ranch, which continued to prosper.

History

In 1887, the house at Bellegrove burned down and consequently Mrs Adair decided to make Glenveagh her principal residence in Ireland. Over the next thirty years, she spent most of her time in Glenveagh where she became a society hostess of note. She is remembered for her acts of kindness and interest in the welfare of the local community. She continually sought to improve the castle's comforts turning what had begun as a comfortable hunting lodge into a spacious building with a country house atmosphere. New wings were added in 1888 to form a courtyard to the front of the castle. These contained the present hall and a large billiard room (now the drawing room) on one side and opposite, a carriage room which now houses the Visitor Reception area for the Castle. The last addition to the Castle was in 1901 when the Round Tower was completed. The middle floor contains a beautifully modelled oval bedroom that was favoured by Mrs Adair and is now known as the Blue Room.

In the 1890's extensive new works were carried out on the Estate. Construction of the 27 mile (45km) deer fence commenced in 1891 and Mrs Adair purchased red deer stocks from Britain and from elsewhere in Ireland. Some years later, she received a gift of a stag from King Edward VII. Woodlands of Scots Pine were planted at Derrylahan, at the lower end of the Glen, and major landscape works were carried out in the Gardens.

Mrs Adair's House Party. August 1901. Standing centre: - Lord Kitchener

The following decade saw a stream of visitors coming to Glenveagh for the deer stalking. The pinnacle of Mrs Adair's entertaining was undoubtedly reached in 1902 when her house parties included the Duke and Duchess of Connaught and Lord Kitchener.

The outbreak of the First World War in 1914 sounded the death-knell for Edwardian country-house living, both here and in Britain. Mrs Adair, who had become a British subject, put Glenveagh to use in the war effort by housing some 30 Belgian war wounded. In gratitude, the refugees constructed a woodland walk above the Pleasure Grounds still known today as the Belgian Walk. Mrs Adair continued to summer at the castle until 1916, but thereafter stayed in England, where she died in 1921 at the age of eighty-two.

In early 1922, during the Civil War that followed Irish independence, the castle was occupied by anti-Treaty forces, who stationed outposts in the gate lodges and used the remote valley as a centre of operations. In July 1922, soldiers of the Free State Army moved on the castle and forced the Irregulars to withdraw. The new occupants remained until 1925.

History

Arthur Kingsley Porter

As the Adairs had no children, the estate had been inherited on her death by Mrs Adair's grandson by her first marriage but by 1925 the condition of the castle had declined considerably. Most of the castle's panelling had been burnt as firewood and little furniture was left in place. The castle and estate was put on the market and, in 1929, was sold to Arthur Kingsley Porter, a Harvard professor of fine arts with a special interest in medieval art and architecture. Kingsley Porter had already spent much of his life in Europe, and he came to Ireland to study Irish archaeology and culture. He and his wife, Lucy, had the castle repaired and redecorated in a modest fashion. A conical roof was added to the round tower and inside, the rooms were painted, the hall was patterned with shells, and some of Mrs Adair's furniture, bought back at auction, was reinstalled.

The Kingsley Porters mainly entertained Irish literary and artistic figures, and a small vestige of their residency is the collection of paintings by Æ (George Russell), whose interest in the Celtic revival and Irish mythology may have been of some help to his host. While staying with his wife on Inishbofin, an island off the Donegal coast in July 1933, Kingsley Porter went out for a walk by the shore one day and never returned. Rumours abounded as to his disappearance, some say he was drowned by a freak wave, others say he was smuggled off the island and started a new life in Paris! Understandably, Donegal held less attraction for Mrs Kingsley Porter thereafter and in 1934 she leased the estate for the summer to other Americans - Mrs McIlhenny of Philadelphia and her son, Henry Plumer McIlhenny. Following a return visit in 1936, Henry McIlhenny took up an option to buy the estate.

John McIlhenny born 1830

Henry's grandfather, John McIlhenny, had been born in Carrigart, Co. Donegal in 1830 and grew up in what is now the Garda Station in nearby Milford. John emigrated to Columbus, Georgia, where he was Mayor for 20 years. His son (also John) built on his father's business interests and became an extremely successful industrialist based in Philadelphia.

John and Frances McIlhenny were keen art collectors, an interest which their son, Henry, developed studying fine art in Harvard University. In 1934, Henry joined the staff of the Philadelphia Museum of Art, where his duties allowed him long summer absences. This greatly facilitated what were to be his annual visits to Glenveagh.

The present appearance of Glenveagh Castle is the result of Henry McIlhenny's continual refinements to it after he bought the Glenveagh Estate in 1937. He strove to soften the castle's outwardly hard and inelegant style by developing lush gardens around it and by adding variety and luxury to its interior. His plans were, however, interrupted by the outbreak of the Second World War in 1939. In 1947, McIlhenny was able to return to Glenveagh and to its redecoration. By the late 1940's, he had begun to buy Victorian paintings, many by Edwin Landseer. Landseer, an English artist was renowned for his paintings of deer, and Henry McIlhenny made a pursuit of acquiring his pictures. In 1956, he bought two of Landseer's greatest works, 'Night' and 'Morning', and eventually owned fifteen of his paintings. These formed a perfect focus for the deer theme that Mr McIlhenny made a central feature of Glenveagh.

History

Henry Plumer McIlhenny

From 1947 until 1983, Mr McIlhenny stayed for several months each year devoting his time to restoring the castle and developing its gardens. He was visited at his remote hide-away by leading figures of international society, including the screen actors Greta Garbo and Grace Kelly, and he carried on the 'Big House' lifestyle until his departure, though it had died out in almost all Irish country houses many years before.

After Henry McIlhenny retired from the Philadelphia Museum of Art in 1964 - immediately becoming a trustee and later chairman of the board - he had even more time to enjoy Glenveagh, and his summer visits often extended to five months. Eventually, he began to find the travelling to and from Ireland too demanding, and the upkeep of the estate was also becoming a strain. In 1975, he agreed the sale of the Glenveagh Estate to the State, allowing for the creation of a National Park. In 1983, he bestowed the castle on the Nation, along with the Gardens. Following this, the castle underwent some essential repairs before being opened to the public in 1986.

Apart from the most important paintings, furniture and silver, which Mr McIlhenny left to the museum in Philadelphia, the contents of the castle remained in place. The colour schemes and arrangements have also been retained. The furniture is a lovely mix of George III, Regency and Victorian, with some pieces from other periods and a number of more unusual items from around the world. The Landseer paintings have been replaced by contemporary engravings and prints of the artist's work. Henry McIlhenny died unexpectedly in Philadelphia in 1986, at the age of 75. Glenveagh National Park opened to the public in 1984, while the Castle was opened in 1986, a few months after its last private owner died.

'Night' by Edwin Landseer

The Castle Interior

Each room in the castle has its own style, colour and décor, designed by Mr McIlhenny to complement their individual functions. A room-by-room account is presented in the sequence these rooms are visited on the guided tour of the Castle.

The Hall

The entrance to Glenveagh Castle is very attractive but surprisingly modest in size. The front door opens into an unimposing barrel-vaulted room, more corridor than hall, with neither the scale nor ceremony one might expect in a castle. Like the narrow corridors throughout the building, the hall is basically functional and has the air of being added on, as indeed it was when Mrs Adair extended a new wing from the keep tower in 1888. Glenveagh was always a summer home to its owners and this is expressed in the hall's shell decorations, which were designed by the Kingsley Porters and crafted by estate-workers Matt Armour and Jimmy Brady early in the 1930's.

Stags' heads introduce the deer theme prominent throughout the house. A pair made from marblised plaster flank the door, while on the wall is a pair of 19th-century carved heads with natural antlers, believed to be of German origin. The blanket chest contained travelling rugs and towels for swimmers.

The Castle Interior

The Music Room

On the ground floor of the round tower, Mr McIlhenny made the music room a light-hearted reminder of the parallels between Glenveagh and Balmoral. Its cloth wall-covering of the Gordon Clan tartan should alert anyone who missed the connection, but the cloth wall-covering was also intended to improve the acoustic properties of the room. Although it no longer has its grand piano, which, when he left Glenveagh, Mr McIlhenny donated to the church in Ramelton where his great grand-parents were married, there is an unusual square piano, and an Irish harp dating from about 1840. The mirror and the chandelier use antlers from various deer species, along with wild boar tusks. Victorian tables of antelope horn and brass, doorstops cast in the form of stags and fruitwood brackets carved as trophies all emphasise the hunting theme.

The Castle Interior

The Drawing Room

The Drawing Room, on the ground floor of the wing added by Mrs Adair, comes as a surprise after the shallow hall. A spacious formal room, its soft colours and rich textures differ sharply from the stark black and white of the entrance hall. It was built as a billiard room and is where most of the socialising took place.

The room was redecorated after the Second World War by Henry McIlhenny who appointed mainly George III furniture, including sofas, chairs, stools and two mahogany bookcases, the larger one with Gothic glazing. The rugs were made in Killybegs to designs copied, at Mr McIlhenny's request, from the English material of the seat covers.

The 18th-century white marble mantelpiece was brought from Ards House, Co. Donegal. To one side of it is an 18th-century pole screen used to shield the wax make-up of the ladies from the heat. It depicts a stag. To the other side is a celestial globe, dated 1876, which most likely at one time had a terrestrial twin. The room also contains a pier glass, an inlaid table, busts of Homer and Mycaenas and a selection of paintings.

The Study

The study - or Red Room - best typifies the air of comfortable formality that pervades the castle. It is a luxurious room, with its deep mahogany and white enveloped by a stately crimson, Henry McIlhenny's favourite colour. It served as both a study and a sitting room. In Mr McIlhenny's time, golden retrievers padded around or slept on a couch by the turf fire.

The fireplace, like several others, came from Ards. The mantelpiece has an inset panel painted to imitate a Byzantine mosaic tile. Above it is an 18th-century walnut and gilt mirror. The room is enriched with gilt and brass, including a pair of mirrors carved as military trophies. An early 19th-century Anglo-Indian table, with masks in place of drawer handles, was introduced by the Kingsley Porters.

Alleviating the richness are some plain white porcelain ornaments, including a pair of elephants supporting obelisks and two pen trays in the shape of tortoises, with their shells as lids. The room contained several Victorian paintings. Above the George III bureau is a reproduction of one, John Calcott Horsley's 'Lovers under a Blossom Tree'.

The Castle Interior

The Dining Room

Without its gleaming abundance of silver - and more so, the guests who gathered here four times each day - the dining room has something of a sparse air. But its decoration was always deliberately spare, depending on a few pieces to give it an appropriately sober elegance.
Here, Mr McIlhenny entertained his guests with warm hospitality and attention to detail. Dinner was always served by candlelight. He continually varied the tableware, and to augment it, commissioned from Salzburg the dinner and tea service laid out here. Its 365 pieces bear a prancing stag coloured in the pale Glenveagh green.

The ochre marble of the mid-18th-century fireplace sets a colour tone for the fabrics, including the printed cotton screen and the Donegal tweed of the seats and curtains. The screen masks an already concealed door cut into the wall, which gives access to the pantry. At the other end of the room a false door on the right answers the entrance symmetrically. The giltwood mirror is of a period with the fireplace. The carpets are Portuguese.

The outstanding feature of this room was a pair of Landseer canvasses, which Mr McIlhenny left to the Philadelphia Museum of Art. A powerful climax to the deer theme at Glenveagh, 'Night' and 'Morning' represent a fatal battle between two great stags. The original paintings have been replaced with reproductions.

The Castle Interior

The Library

The library, situated on the first floor of the keep and above the study, was mainly used as a daytime sitting room, offering fine views across the lake and along the valley. Mr McIlhenny added to its decoration while retaining much of what was left there by Kingsley Porter. These include the four paintings by Æ (George Russell).

18th-century Irish tables stand in the window bays, their dark mahogany colour picking up the other dark furniture - a big bookcase, a lacquered Italian box and teabin lamps. In the corner, over a George III bureau, is a 15th-century Italian carved saint.

The Tuscan Garden, flanked by August-flowering Eucryphia trees, was designed to be viewed from this room.

The Castle Interior

The Master Bedroom

Like the study, this room is an essay in crimson and mahogany. Most of the furniture is Regency, including the mahogany four-poster bed, which Mrs Kingsley Porter brought to Glenveagh. In the corner to the left is a small architect's table with a hinged top. The armchairs and big wardrobe are Victorian. The Landseer print above the fireplace, 'The Hunted Stag', replaces a more peaceful painting that Henry McIlhenny had hanging here.

The all white en suite bathroom was converted from a bedroom in the 1960s, when Mr McIlhenny panelled the walls with shutters from Ards. Above the fireplace, also from Ards, hang three steel engravings after Canova's copies of statues in the Vatican - the Apollo, Belvedere and Hercules. The chandeliers of Venetian glass, are modern.

The Master Bathroom

The Castle Interior

The Pink Room

In each storey of the round tower is an oval room within the circle, with corridors, cupboards or bathrooms fitted into the space left over. Forming the top floor of the round tower, the Pink Bedroom has an oriental air, with some of the furnishings being inlaid with mother-of-pearl in the Chinese style of which the Victorians were so fond. The room's mirrors are inlaid in this way and decorated with gilt Chinese designs. Most of the small pieces of lacquered or ebonised furniture are made of papier-mâché and give an idea of the variety of items that were pressed from this material in the 19th century, including chairs, stools, nests, dressing-tables, mirrors, clocks, lockers and cabinets. This method began as a cheaper version of the Chinese lacquered furniture that appeared in Europe in the 17th century.

The bedroom was originally partitioned and housed two maids. Since one of them would have enjoyed better views than some of the guests, the room was duly converted into a guest room.

The Blue Room

On the first floor of the round tower, the Blue Room has an alcove extending from the oval containing a bathroom and wardrobe. The cleverness of the arrangement is enhanced by the fire, whose flue runs around the window above it. However, the engineering never matched the idea and the fire always drew poorly, often filling the room with smoke.

The bedroom - furnished in an American style - is blue in colour, which is said to have been Mrs Adair's choice. Its lightness in tone is mirrored in pale oak and satinwood furniture, including a Victorian davenport, American beds and the sofa table in the alcove. Around the walls are gouache sketches of the Pantheon, the Trevi Fountain and other monuments in Rome, a city where, for a time, Henry McIlhenny worked at the American Academy.

The Bachelors' Corridor

Three bedrooms open off of this corridor, which as the name suggests, would have accommodated un-married male guests. On the walls of the corridor are a series of paintings by Carroll Sargent Tyson. Born on 23rd November 1877, Tyson specialised in paintings of birds and landscapes. Exhibitions of his works were held in New York, Boston, Philadelphia, Washington D.C and London. He died on 19th March 1956.

The Back Stairs leads to what was once the Carriage House. The upper floor was used as a staff sleeping quarters. Latterly the downstairs was split in two: a gun room and the flower room. This now houses the Visitor Reception area.

Glenveagh Castle Gardens

Introduction

Perhaps nowhere in Ireland is there such a remarkable contrast between the Garden as a work of art and the rugged and exposed natural landscape than at Glenveagh. The Gardens, which surround the Castle, cover an area of 32 acres (13 hectares) and contain a rich and varied plant collection. There are over 1200 different plant species and varieties in all, representative of the temperate flora of different parts of the world. Glenveagh is perhaps best known for its Rhododendrons as well as tender exotic species from the Mediterranean, Asia, especially the Himalayan region, Australia, Tasmania, New Zealand and South America, notably Chile.

Foxtail Lilies *Eremurus* along the Woods Path (Walled Garden)

Development of the Gardens

The site of the Castle had been chosen for its commanding view of Lough Veagh and early photographs show the Castle dominating the Glen. Later, after additions had been made to the Castle by Mrs Adair in 1888, she decided that the area around the castle should be landscaped into gardens. An enclosing fence was erected protecting the Garden area from the newly introduced deer, shelterbelts of Scots Pine and *Rhododendron ponticum* were planted and major landscape works got underway. It is at this point (c. 1890) that the Pleasure Grounds and Kitchen Garden were added as we see them today.

Development of the Gardens

The two-acre (one hectare) lawn was laid out by draining and levelling an area of bog northeast of the Castle. Great quantities of topsoil were imported to set a lawn. This came to be known as the Pleasure Grounds whose borders were planted with flowering trees and shrubs. Plants that survive from the original planting include the tree rhododendrons – *Rhododendron falconeri* and *Rh. arboreum*, Purple Japanese Maple, Japanese Cedar, Chusan Palms, Cordyline, Griselinia, Chilean Lantern tree and, of course, the very invasive *Rhododendron ponticum*. Photographs in Mrs Adair's visitors book show guests enjoying the outdoor environment in a well-established garden by 1902.

The Lawn and Castle c.1902

At the same time, a Kitchen Garden was established and a gardener's house built. The format of the Kitchen Garden, with its six plots divided by paths and surrounded by herbaceous borders all date from this period. The Kitchen Garden was later surrounded by walls by Henry McIlhenny (c.1959-60). Oral history relates that the site of the Kitchen Garden (now known as the Walled Garden) was originally the quarry site from which the stone for the construction of the Castle was extracted.

The wonderful deep black soil of the Walled Garden plots has been carefully nurtured and cultivated by generations of gardeners. A tradition of soil husbandry evolved in the early days of the garden and continues to this day. Each autumn when the vegetable crops are harvested, the soil is manured, trenched and made into ridges two feet (66 cm.) high. This practice, which seem to be unique to Glenveagh, is ideal for a garden where rainfall is high and the growing season is short. In the spring, when the season for planting-out new crops has arrived (mid-March to mid-May) these ridges are levelled – the free draining soil having already been warmed by the sun is ready for immediate planting.

Development of the Gardens

Dahlia 'Matt Armour'

Matt Armour (left) with Henry McIlhenny

In the short time that the Kingsley Porters owned Glenveagh, (1929-1934) Lucy Kingsley Porter took an interest in the garden. Perhaps her most important contribution was of some dahlia seed, which she gave to Matt Armour (then a young gardener). From this seed he raised the unique single red dahlia, which today bears his name, Dahlia 'Matt Armour'. This is still in cultivation in the Walled Garden and is unique to Glenveagh.

Mr McIlhenny had a small staff taking care of Glenveagh during the years of the Second World War. His head gardener, Matt Armour and Jim Gamble on hearing of Henry McIlhenny's return in 1947, hand dug the two acre lawn and re-seeded it so that it would be in a presentable state on their master's return.

In the late 1940's the very fine Victorian framework of the Gardens created between 1890-1900 was still very much intact. Their transformation, into one of Ireland's foremost gardens, imaginatively designed and supporting a rich variety of rare and tender plants, was the work of Henry McIlhenny, who personally supervised their development from 1947 until 1983.

In 1947, the Gardens presented a daunting challenge, with *Rhododendron ponticum* and bamboo run wild, though some exceptional plants of earlier plantings still remained. The Belgian Walk had also survived. Mr McIlhenny began collecting plants from all over the world. To begin with, many new and unusual plants were bought from the Leitrim Estate at Mulroy in North Donegal. Lady Ann Leitrim, a friend of McIlhenny and well-known plantswoman, helped with advice on the development of the Gardens. McIlhenny's own knowledge of plants and his sense of artistry were later augmented by expert landscaping advice, initially from James Russell and then from Lanning Roper.

A renowned English nurseryman, James Russell came to work in Glenveagh in 1953. Russell advised that Cornelia Adair's rhododendron collection be expanded. His two-themed approach was to plant large-leafed rhododendrons for their noble form and scented rhododendrons for their fragrance. The latter are often tender, but the milder microclimate of the Gardens has suited *Rhododendron* 'Polar Bear', *Rh. ciliatum, Rh. lindleyi* and others.

Lanning Roper was born in New Jersey and studied in Harvard with Henry McIlhenny before settling in England. Regarded as one of the outstanding garden designers of his time, he had a major involvement in the development of the Castle Gardens between 1961 and 1982. Other Irish gardens where he advised with landscape design include Trinity College Dublin, Castlecoole in Co. Fermanagh, and Marble Hill, Co. Donegal.

Development of the Gardens

The plans of Russell and Roper were implemented by Glenveagh estate staff; particularly Matt Armour who had came to Glenveagh in 1930 and served as head gardener throughout the McIlhenny years until 1983. The creation of the formal elements in the Gardens began with the neo-Gothic orangery built in 1957 to designs by Philippe Julian, a French cultural historian. The Tuscan Garden followed in 1958 (below the Castle) complete with classical statues and marble busts. The walls of the Rose and View Gardens and their Summer Houses were built in 1959. The Flag Yard (adjacent to today's Tea-rooms) was laid out in 1965. The Italian Terrace on the Belgian Walk above the Pleasure Grounds followed in 1966. In 1967, Russell made creative use of a rocky gully carpeted with mosses and ferns under a canopy of oak, which descends the hillside behind the Castle. A scenic stone path up the gully was completed and along one side a steep flight of 67 stone steps was constructed leading to a high, grassy viewpoint which overlooks the Castle and the Gardens in their lakeside setting.

Mr McIlhenny replanted the Belgian Walk, the Twelve Step Path and the View Garden. Along the lakeshore to the south of the castle, he created the Swiss Walk leading to the Tuscan Garden. He enhanced the exotic nature of the Pleasure Grounds by adding tree ferns, palms and rhododendrons and he provided ground cover with beds of *Gunnera, Astilbe, Bergenia, Hosta* and lilies, the latter being one of his specialities. Each year crates of Lily bulbs would arrive from the famous Oregon Bulb Farm for fresh planting through the garden.

The Walled Garden, Spring 1998

Development of the Gardens

By the 1970's the Castle Gardens had developed into a sophisticated combination of classical and contemporary design, with a rich and varied plant collection. Mr McIlhenny planted the Gardens for effect rather than to show off individual plants. He gave each section of the Gardens its own character and style and linked them all together with winding paths. With clever planning, the Gardens feature a range of plants that create interest and colour throughout the year. However, he was particularly pleased with his late-flowering plants, including several fine specimens of *Hoheria* and *Eucryphia*. At all times of the year, the rugged grandeur of the setting contrasts vividly with the studied luxuriance of the plantings, and this remains the Gardens' greatest distinction.

Since Mr McIlhenny's departure in 1983, the unique character of the Gardens has been conserved by maintaining the particular range of plants which he left within it and by the sympathetic addition of new plants. Recent additions to the plant collection include new species of Rhododendron, from northwest Yunnan, a province in southern China and a collection of endangered tree and shrub species donated by the Royal Botanic Gardens, Edinburgh.

Scots Pine shelter-belt and exotic planting in the Pleasure Grounds 1985

The Garden Trail

The trail follows the route favoured by Henry McIlhenny while taking guests around. It takes about an hour to see all the features, however you can return to the Castle at several points should time only allow for a short visit. It is worth noting that each separate area of the garden has been given a particular landscape treatment, furnished with plants of a particular texture, colour range and growth pattern. The trail begins just inside the main gates to the Pleasure Grounds.

1. The idea of the **Pleasure Grounds** became popular in the Victorian period. Completely separate from the Kitchen Garden where food was produced for the Castle table, the Pleasure Grounds was an area in the garden where the guests of the "Big House" could take the air and enjoy the outdoor environment at leisure. One of the games which guests played here for their entertainment was croquet. Above and below the path at this point are the Purple Japanese Maple, Tree Ferns and the Chusan Palm. These are under planted with *Hosta, Bergenia, Primula, Cornus alba* 'Elegantissima' and Corokia cotoneaster.

② Passing under the fine Katsura Tree, you come to the Himalayan tree rhododendrons such as *Rhododendron falconeri* (with crimson bark and rust colour on the undersurface of the leaf) and the Japanese bamboo, *Sasa palmata*, Rhododendrons and bamboos are some of the characteristic plants of the Castle Gardens. Follow the path that crosses the lawn to the left.

③ The fine expanse of lawn provides the ideal foil to the exotic planting that borders it. The enormous rhubarb like plant is *Gunnera tinctoria*, which is native to Chile. Bordering the lawn opposite are fine examples of *Trachycarpus fortunei* (Chusan Palm), *Trochodendron araloides* and *Rhododendron sinograndi* making an interesting tapestry of leaf texture. Follow the path crossing the lawn and around to the right.

The Garden Trail

④ Looking across the lawn away from the **Balinese statues** to the planting on the far side, you can see a rich textural arrangement of trees, shrubs and herbaceous plants. The Tasmanian tree ferns (*Dicksonia antartica*) lend an exotic air to the theme that includes fine specimens of the southern beech, *Nothofagus obliqua* and *N. cliffortioides*. Nearby are *Magnolia salicifolia* from Japan and *M. tripetala* from NE America. Bordering the lawn are the Azalea 'Superba' flowering in late May and early June, and a host of herbaceous plants that include *Hosta* 'Elegantissima', *Astilbe*, *Aruncus*, *Phormium*, *Lysichiton* and *Rodgersia*. The borders on this side of the lawn are planted with a silver-grey and purple foliage theme. Follow the path to the end of the lawn.

The Garden Trail

⑤ This view looking back over the lawn resembles the view of the lake and surrounding hills. The large evergreen tree with twisting trunk and branches in *Cryptomeria japonica* 'Elegans'. Along with the fine specimen of *Acer palmatum* 'Atropurpureum', these are some of the first introductions to the garden between 1890 and 1900.

The trail passes through the gates and goes right at the next junction. To the right is an excellent example of *Michelia doltsopa* – which produces white fragrant tulip like flowers in spring. The Garden Trail takes the next right turn under the full-grown evergreen *Griselinia littoralis*, a native of Australia planted here around 1900.

⑥ Stopping under the 90-ft (30 m.) tall pine trees, *Pinus nigra*, and looking up to the left you will see a view crowned with a stone pillar topped with a stone-carved pineapple. The pineapple is a symbol of hospitality – something that was important to Henry McIlhenny, whose generosity as a host is remembered by the many people who visited the Castle. A few metres further on, a narrow path to the left leads to a viewpoint on a rocky knoll. This charming woodland walk, known as the Twelve Step Walk, is planted with *Pseudowintera*, *Fasicularia* and *Rhododendron johnstoneanum*. It is highly recommended but you will have to retrace your steps to continue the trail.

(7) You are now on the **Belgian Walk,** so called because it was made by Belgian convalescent soldiers, housed at Glenveagh by Mrs Adair during the First World War. The steep slope to the left is planted with the early flowering *Rhododendron ciliatum*. To the right are good specimens of the late flowering *Eucryphia moorei*, a southeast Australian evergreen rarely seen in Irish Gardens, together with *Magnolia hypoleuca* from Japan. Further on is the early flowering *Eucryphia lucida* from Tasmania.

Rhododendron ciliatum Blossoms

Rhododendron ciliatum

Glenveagh Castle Gardens

The Garden Trail

⑧ The **Italian Terrace** is one of the last of the classical elements to be added to the Castle Gardens. It was constructed in 1966 from local stone and furnished with iron seats made by local craftsmen. The 19th century Italian statues on plinths depict Bacchus and Ganymede. The terracotta pots from the famous Imprunata pottery outside Florence are planted with hosta and azaleas. The columnar habit of the Italian Cypress, *Cupressus sempervirens* 'Stricta', adds to the Italianate atmosphere. Opposite is a fine specimen of *Metrosideros umbellata*, an evergreen tree from New Zealand that is covered with bright red flowers in July.

⑨ Continuing along the **Belgian Walk** to the left you pass the red flowered *Rhododendron* 'Mulroy Vanguard' and on the right the Chilean conifer *Podocarpus salignus*. At the bend in the path, the Hindu God Ganesh overlooks the pond. This area is known as the Himalayan Garden because of the predominance of large-leafed tree Rhododendrons, *Rhododendron protistum, Rh. mollyanum* and *Rh. macabeanum*. This mix of Oak, Birch and Rhododendron is similar to the broadleaf forests that cling to the slopes of the great Himalayan range. Follow the path around to the right.

The Italian Terrace Inset: Bacchus (left) and Ganymede (right)

The Garden Trail

10 Further along the path to the left a rocky bank is planted with a South American bromeliad called *Fasicularia bicolor*. The inner leaves of each crown turn a dramatic red in autumn, setting off a disc of pale blue flowers at its centre. At Stop 10 you are standing under a fine specimen of *Nothofagus dombeyii*, a native to Chile and Argentina. This specimen was planted here in the early 1960's and is an evergreen relative of the European beech tree. Beneath it grows the Japanese *Rhododendron yakushimanum* – its leaves have a felt-like undersurface, presumably to reduce water loss.

11 The **Walled Garden** is the centrepiece of the Castle Gardens. The layout of six plots divided by paths is original and dates from around 1890. Here a broad range of vegetables, fruit, herbs and flowers are grown together in a style known as the Jardin Potager. This ornamental style utilizes culinary vegetables as well as flowers for ornamental display. The surrounding herbaceous borders are filled with traditional perennial flowers, many of which have been in cultivation at Glenveagh for many years. These include *Delphinium, Lupin, Phlox, Geranium, Iris, Papaver* and *Paeonia*. The single red flowered *Dahlia* 'Matt Armour' was first raised at Glenveagh in the 1930's and is unique to Glenveagh. The well-known Irish apple variety *Malus* 'Irish Peach' can be seen, as can the old-fashioned fodder cabbage from Gortahork, Co. Donegal. The trail follows the path around the top of the Walled Garden past the Dolphin Fountain.

The Garden Trail

12 Vistas and views have been created throughout the Garden. Here, the Plum, Apple and Pear trees frame the view of the Castle and the Gothic Orangery. The Orangery was designed specially for Glenveagh by the French architect Philippe Jullian. Inside are grown tender exotic species such as *Jasminum, Plumbago*, Passion flower, Bird of Paradise and Lemon trees. The woodland above the Walled Garden is planted with Azaleas and a range of tender plants.

13 To the left, the **Rose Garden** is planted with mostly shrub roses (*Rosa rugosa* 'Hansa', 'Scabrosa', 'Roserie de la Hay', 'Queen of Denmark', 'Albertine' and 'Ballerina') that are tolerant of the high rainfall and cool temperatures of Glenveagh. There is also a small collection of cottage garden roses collected from old homesteads around Co. Donegal. The two gazebos, built around 1959-60, are roofed with shingles made from pine trees grown at Glenveagh.

The Garden Trail

(14) As you leave the Rose Garden passing into the View Garden, stop to take in the effect of the light reflected on the foliage of the planting in this area. Most of the shrubs and trees in this area are glossy leafed, (*Ilex, Elaeagnus, Oleria, Senecio, Cotoneaster*) and were planted together here to create a shimmering effect when the sun is out or, indeed, when the moon is bright. Just before the Trembling Aspen tree (*Populus tremula*) in the centre of the path, are steps and a gate leading to a woodland walk from where the 67 Steps may be viewed.

The Garden Trail turns to the right, before the circular lawn, past *Magnolia wilsonii* and *Rhododendron* 'Shilsonii'. It then crosses the road to the lower Glen and through the Gate with pillars supporting lead Urns.

(15) You are now in an area known as the Swiss Walk. Just inside the gate you pass *Nothofagus fusca* and *Brachyglottis hectoris* on your right and a large specimen of the late flowering *Rhododendron* 'Polar Bear' on your left. Follow the path to your left.

16 Passing under a canopy of Scots Pine, Holly and Southern Beech, under-planted with Azaleas, you arrive at a viewing point with a seat. Here Henry McIlhenny found his favourite spot in the Garden.

17 From this point there is a fine view up the Glen. At the end of the lake is a sandy beach and the small white speck above it is the hunting lodge in the Upper Glen. On the hillside to the left of the lake is Mullangore Wood. These woods are very special because they represent an ancient remnant of the once extensive native Oak forests (*Quercus petraea*). A major conservation programme involving the removal of the invasive *Rhododendron ponticum* from these woods has been under way since the 1970's. In the hills above, the Golden Eagle has recently been reintroduced to the Park from Scotland in the hope that pairs will eventually breed and establish a native population once again in Ireland.

In this area of the Garden are planted *Rhododendron luteum* – flowering in early May and *Olearia x hastii* flowering in summer. A short walk on the path in front of you leads to the **Chinese Heath** - a new plantation of Chinese Alpine Rhododendrons.

The Garden Trail

(18) Returning to the Swiss Walk and along the lakeshore the path takes you back to the Castle. Below the great square tower of the Castle is the **Tuscan Garden**. Created about 1958, it is the most important formal element in the Castle Gardens. The rectangular lawn is lined with *Griselinia* hedges. Life size statues of Bacchus and Cornucopia adorn the lower end together with a stone bench and a pair of classical urns. The upper end being guarded with a pair of Sphinx. Here the blue-flowered *Rhododendron augustinii* blooms in spring followed by the red-flowered *Crinodendron hookerianum* in June. In late summer the white-flowered *Eucryphia* is in full bloom (*E. cordifolia, E. glutinosa, E. x nymansensis* 'Nymansay'). Six marble busts of Roman Emperors and their wives line the sides of the Tuscan Garden.

The path leads up to the Castle terrace, where the scale of the building is at its most impressive. Looking across the lake, a small area of woodland has been enclosed with a fence since the early 1980's, to prevent grazing by deer. The resulting regeneration of heather and young trees is now evident. Below you, at the lake edge, is the boathouse. The view from above the boathouse is particularly fine.

You have now reached the end of the Garden Trail. You can return to the Castle Reception via the Castle lawn. From there you will find the tearooms, toilets and other facilities. We hope you have enjoyed your visit.

The Tuscan Garden Inset: Bacchus (left) Cornucopia (centre) Bearded Angel (right)